Nature's Children

CARIBOU

El Segundo Public Library

Judy Ross

GROLIER
EDUCATIONAL

FACTS IN BRIEF

Classification of the caribou
  Class: *Mammalia* (mammals)
  Order: *Artiodactyla* (cloven-hoofed mammals)
  Family: *Cervidae* (deer family)
  Genus: *Rangifer*
  Species: *Rangifer tarandus*

World distribution.   Northern regions of North America, Europe and Asia.

Habitat.   Arctic tundra and/or coniferous forest.

Distinctive physical characteristics.   Antlers on both males and females; small ears and tail; large feet; coloration varies with subspecies.

Habits.   Live in small bands or larger herds, depending on the time of year; are active during the day; barren-ground caribou migrate often and over great distances.

Diet.   Lichens, mushrooms, grasses, twigs, shrubs.

Published originally as
"Getting to Know . . . Nature's Children."

This series is approved and recommended
by the Federation of Ontario Naturalists.

This library reinforced edition is available exclusively from:

GROLIER
EDUCATIONAL
Sherman Turnpike, Danbury, Connecticut 06816

Contents

If you think that caribou look a lot like Santa's reindeer, you are right. Reindeer is the name given to caribou that live in Russia, Norway, Sweden and Finland. There, reindeer are raised as domestic animals, and many of them are really used for pulling sleds.

You might easily mistake a caribou for a very large deer. That is understandable, because the caribou is a member of the deer family. A baby caribou looks very much like a baby deer—except that it does not have white spots.

The antlers of the barren-ground caribou are larger than those of their woodland cousins.

Meet the Baby

This caribou baby, called a fawn, has already survived the most dangerous time in its young life—the first few hours after birth. Because it lives in a herd, it must be able to keep up with the group. If it gets left behind it could easily be caught by a wolf. This is why the mother caribou licks and nuzzles her newborn to encourage it to get up on its wobbly legs as soon as possible.

You were probably about one year old when you started walking. But this caribou fawn could stand up when it was only one hour old! In less than two hours, it was strong enough to walk several kilometres. Caribou fawns are fast as well as strong. A day-old fawn could run faster than a man!

Deer Relatives

The caribou is part of a very large family—the deer family. Some relatives that live in the caribou's neighborhood are the White-tailed Deer, the Mule Deer, the elk and the moose. All these deer relatives share certain features.

All of them have split hoofs, and none of them has any top front teeth. In addition, they are all cud chewers. This means they swallow food whole and store it in a special part of their stomach until they are ready to bring it back into their mouths and chew it.

But the most obvious similarity among deer family members is their antlers. All males grow and shed a new set of antlers every year. Unlike many of their deer relatives, the female caribou usually grows antlers too.

As a caribou's antlers grow, they are covered with a furry skin known as velvet.

Caribou Country

There are two kinds of caribou in North America. One kind lives in forests and mountains. These are called woodland caribou. The others, called the barren-ground caribou, live on the frozen tundra of the far north.

The woodland caribou does not live as far north as its cousin, but winters in its forest home can be cold too.

The barren-ground caribou live where the winters are long and harsh. The cold often lasts for nine months. During this time, the ground is covered with snow, and the rivers and lakes are frozen over.

Where caribou can be found in North America.

Keeping Warm

The caribou has many ways of keeping warm in winter.

It has a special double-thick fur coat to keep body heat in and the cold and wet out. The long outer guard hairs are hollow. They contain air, which provides some insulation, and they lie flat against the caribou's body to form a shield against rain and snow. Under the guard hairs is a thick crinkly underfur which traps the air warmed by the caribou's body.

You know how cold your nose can get on a winter day. The caribou is not bothered by a cold nose. Its nose is completely covered with hair. Every part of the caribou's body is furry, even its ears and tail. The caribou's ears and tail are tiny for such a big animal. That way less body heat is lost through them.

The coat of the caribou is longer and denser than that of other deer.

Changing Coats

You would not want to wear your winter coat all year long, would you? Of course not. In summer you would be too hot.

The caribou does not wear its thick coat all year long either. It sheds it in great clumps in the early summer. Although the caribou looks tattered and patchy during this molt, it is never bald. A new lightweight coat grows in as the old winter coat falls out.

Both the woodland and the barren-ground caribou are mostly brown, with white markings on their legs, belly, neck and tail. The woodland caribou are generally a dark chocolate brown, while the barren-ground caribou are a lighter, clove color.

Old bulls, like the one in the center of this picture can be identified by their white mane.

Fabulous Feet

The caribou's feet are well designed for walking in deep snow. Its large hoofs splay out as it walks to spread its body weight over a bigger surface—a little bit as snowshoes support a person's weight.

Ice is not a problem either. In winter the horny edge around the outside of the hoof grows. This helps the caribou dig its hoofs into ice, almost as if it was wearing cleats. At the same time, the pads in the center of the hoof shrink and become hard and horny. This way they are less likely to be cut by hardened snow and ice. And hair grows between the caribou's toes, forming a warm covering over the pad.

In summer the fleshy pads on the caribou's feet balloon up in size. This gives the caribou lots of support as it walks over soft, marshy ground.

Caribou hoofs.

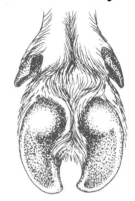

Summer

Winter

There's nothing dainty about a caribou's feet!

Up Close

If a caribou were to stand beside its enormous relative, the moose, it would look pretty small. But an average male woodland caribou, called a buck, weighs about 225 kilograms (500 pounds). The female, or doe, is quite a bit smaller.

Barren-ground caribou are considerably smaller than their woodland cousins. An average buck weighs about 110 kilograms (240 pounds). That is half the weight of its cousin.

The size of the caribou depends on the area where it lives. In areas where there is plenty of food, the caribou are bigger. Where food is scarce, the caribou are smaller. Since it is more difficult to find food in the frozen north, it is not surprising that the barren-ground caribou are generally smaller.

Scratching these antlers is no easy task.

Living Together

You will hardly ever see a caribou on its own. Caribou are sociable animals and live in small bands or large herds, depending on their type and the time of year.

The woodland caribou live in family bands that are usually made up of fewer than 50 animals. These bands change during the year. Sometimes males of the same age form a band and females another band. Usually it is only at mating season that bands of females and males join.

The barren-ground caribou live in large herds made up of thousands of animals.

On the Move

Some animals have homes in which they spend much of their lives. But not the caribou. They are wanderers, on the move most of the year. In the summer they move from pasture to pasture in search of food. In the fall, they head for well-forested areas where they can find protection from the cold and snow. And in spring they travel to special birthing grounds where the young are born.

Generally woodland caribou travel less than barren-ground caribou. The woodland animals often move deeper into the forests or down mountains in the fall, but it is their more northerly cousins who are the real wanderers.

The barren-ground caribou may travel up to 1300 kilometres (800 miles) between winter feeding grounds and summer birthing grounds. They have special routes which they use every year on these migrations.

If you ran as fast as you could you might keep up with walking caribou—until you ran out of breath.

A Noisy Brown Sea

People who have been lucky enough to see a large herd of barren-ground caribou migrating are amazed by the sight. They say it looks like a sea of animals passing by.

As they walk or run the caribou's legs make an odd clicking sound. This is caused when part of one leg rubs against another. On top of this clicking is the sound of antlers clashing. This clicking and clashing can sometimes be heard quite a distance away. And if there are young caribou fawns in the herd, another sound adds to the noise—loud bawling.

Caribou sometimes travel in single file, following a leader along a narrow path. Some herds are so large that it takes days for all the caribou to pass!

Follow the leader.

Running and Swimming

Sometimes a herd of caribou just pokes along, but if they are alarmed, they can gallop at speeds of up to 65 kilometres (40 miles) per hour. But even their normal walking speed is a lot faster than yours.

When migrating, caribou often have to cross wide rivers or lakes. This is no problem because they are strong swimmers. Their wide hoofs make good paddles, and their hollow, air-filled guard hairs act like a life jacket to help keep them afloat.

Caribou often cross lakes and rivers during their annual migration.

Curious Caribou

We all think of cats as being curious animals, but did you know caribou are curious too? They do not seem to be able to resist unusual sights, such as a man waving his arms. They will run off so that they are out of danger then turn and stare. Sometimes they will even come back for a closer look.

Even then, their curiosity may not be fully satisfied and they may try to move downwind of whatever it was that caught their attention. That is because they depend above all on their keen sense of smell to give them information about what is around them.

"Who are you?"

Finding Food

Caribou eat as they walk, browsing on willow shoots and nipping green buds off shrubs and leaves off plants. But the mainstay of their diet is lichen, a low-growing plant that clings to rocks and trees. The average barren-ground caribou can eat about four and a half kilograms (10 pounds) of lichen a day. For a real gourmet treat caribou eat mushrooms.

In winter, when the ground is covered in snow, the caribou eat the twigs of willow and birch trees or dig down with their hoofs to find frozen bits of plants beneath the snow. They rely on their strong sense of smell to find lichen and dried horsetails buried under the snow.

Sometimes in winter caribou even munch on muskrat dens. These are made of dried plants and grasses. Good food for a caribou, but what a surprise for the muskrat!

After feeding the caribou looks for a comfortable resting place and settles down to chew its cud.

Tear, Swallow, Grind

The caribou cannot bite off leaves or bits of lichen because it does not have any top front teeth. Instead it has a rough plate on the roof of its mouth, and it tears off pieces of food. In the back of its mouth are a set of flattened teeth called molars, perfect for grinding up tough plants.

The caribou does not chew its food right away. It swallows lichen, leaves and buds whole and stores them in one part of its stomach. Later it finds a nice spot to lie down. As it relaxes it brings the food, or cud, back to its mouth and grinds it up into a pulp. This is why caribou, like other deer, are called cud chewers.

Danger!

Grizzly Bears, lynx and wolverines will all attack caribou, but wolves are their main enemy. Groups of wolves often follow a herd of caribou, waiting to catch a calf or a sick or old member of the herd. Only occasionally will they catch a healthy adult. By keeping the caribou numbers down, the wolves are actually helping the herd. Since they take the weaker members, there is more food for the stronger ones, who are better able to survive.

When a caribou senses danger it lifts its head high with its ears pointing up and forward, raises its tail and holds one leg out to the side. This rather odd-looking pose warns other caribou "Watch out—danger is near!" If the caribou that has given the alarm suddenly starts to run off, all the others will run too, whether they have seen the enemy or not.

Sometimes a frightened caribou will rear up on its hind legs just like a horse. When it does this its hoofs spread apart and a special scent is deposited on the ground. Other caribou know that this smell means "Watch out!"

Opposite page:

An alert caribou often sniffs the air to check for any strange scent that might betray the presence of an enemy.

Pesky Pests

Wolves may be the biggest danger to the caribou, but flies and mosquitoes cause them the most bother. In the summer the ground where barren-ground caribou live is soggy, and there are many streams and ponds where black flies and mosquitoes breed. Being bitten is an annoying but inevitable way of life for northern animals.

Unfortunately the caribou's lightweight summer coat is not thick enough to protect it from bites. And its tail is not long enough to use as a fly swatter. All a caribou can do is snort with irritation and try to outrun these airborne pests. Sometimes caribou will wear themselves out trying to avoid being bitten.

When the insects are in full force, the caribou often climb up high hills or mountains to find a breezy spot with fewer bugs. If they are still being bothered, they will even plunge into freezing cold northern waters to escape.

On the run.

Mating Time

Caribou mate in October and early November.

A woodland buck gathers a harem of a dozen or more does. For the rest of the mating season, he will spend much of his time rushing around trying to keep them together and fighting off any other buck that tries to get near them.

Barren-ground males do not gather harems. Instead they mate at random in their large herds.

Mating season is a time of great activity for the males of both caribou types. They duel with other males, bellow loudly and sometimes even thrash their antlers around in a thicket of bushes. Before mating season caribou bucks are fat and sleek looking. But they lose weight during the mating season because they do not have much time to eat. When winter comes they are often tired and tattered looking.

Head to head combat.

New Life in Spring

After the long cold winter, spring is very welcome in caribou country. The days are getting longer and warmer, and the does are almost ready to give birth.

Most caribou have special birthing grounds where they go to have their young. If she is traveling with a herd, the mother simply drops behind the group when it is time to have her fawn.

The fawns are born in mid-May to early June. Usually just one fawn is born, but occasionally there may be two or three. The fawn is long legged and reddish brown in color. It weighs about four and a half to six kilograms (10 to 13 pounds). That is about as much as a medium-sized dog.

The mother is very protective. She licks and cleans her baby and cuddles and nudges it constantly. When it has rested, she gently shoves it so that it will stand up and start walking.

The young fawn seems to be all legs!

A Fine Fawn

The fawn's hind legs look very wobbly and bent at first, but soon they straighten out. Before long it can keep up with its mother and the rest of its band or herd. And it can swim too!

Like most babies, fawns love to explore and meet other youngsters. Sometimes one will wander away and get lost. Then the mother goes after her fawn. She can tell it from a group of other look-alike fawns by its scent.

These active babies grow so fast that they double their birth weight in just 10 days. They begin to graze on a few choice bits of greenery after about two weeks, but continue to drink their mother's milk for at least a month. If the weather is very harsh the mother will continue to nurse her fawn for a longer period.

Caribou fawns sprout antlers during their first autumn.

On the Move Again

Often mother caribou with fawns of the same age gather together in a band. That way they can set a speed that the fawns can keep up with.

By fall the fawn will be about five months old and starting to grow its first set of antlers. Soon its mother will be getting ready to mate again. And it will be time to move to more sheltered winter areas.

The fawn will probably stay with its mother through the winter but will go off with other year-old fawns when the new group of babies are born in the spring.

Few caribou live to be older than four or five in the wild. While that might seem like a very short life to us, it is time for a caribou to have several young of its own and walk thousands of kilometres (miles) in its never-ending wanderings.

Words to Know

Buck Male caribou.

Cud Hastily swallowed food brought back for chewing by cud chewers such as cows and caribou.

Doe Female caribou.

Fawn Young caribou.

Guard hairs Long coarse hairs that make up the outer layer of a caribou's coat.

Harem Group of does that a buck gathers together at mating time.

Hoofs Feet of caribou, deer, cattle and some other animals.

Lichen A flowerless moss-like plant that grows on rocks and trees.

Mate To come together to produce young.

Migrate To travel regularly in search of feeding or birthing grounds.

Molt To shed fur and grow new fur, usually at a change of seasons.

Nurse To drink milk from a mother's body.

Tine Prong of a caribou's antlers.

Tundra Flat land in the arctic where no trees grow.

Velvet Soft skin that covers a caribou's antlers while they grow.

INDEX

Cover Photo: Brian Milne (First Light Associated Photographers)

Photo Credits: Stephen J. Krasemann (Valan Photos), pages 4, 8, 11, 15, 19, 22, 25, 30, 34, 37, 38; Fred Bruemmer, page 7; J.D. Taylor (Miller Services), pages 13, 33, 41; J.D. Markou (Miller Services), page 16; Mike Beedele (Miller Services), page 26; Patrick Morrow (First Light Associated Photographers), page 29; Wayne Lankinen (Valan Photos), pages 42, 45.

Printed and Bound in Italy by Lego SpA